THE TAX BILL.

SPEECH

OF

WILLIAM SPRAGUE

IN THE

SENATE OF THE UNITED STATES

APRIL 8, 1869.

THE TAX BILL.

Mr. President: It is not my intention to confine myself strictly to a discussion of the measure before the Senate. I observed, a moment since, that the effect on the distiller and manufacturer of whisky of compelling him to withdraw his whisky before it had ripened for sale, would be injurious to him. I did not say that it would invite speculation, but such will be the result of it. The compelling of a manufacturer to raise large sums of money at this time, at an exorbitant rate of interest, is an oppression toward that manufacturer, and that assertion can not be gainsaid. The effect of placing upon the market large amounts of this commodity will certainly be to depress for a time the market, and there are those who stand ready to seize that favorable opportunity, based upon the distress and the misfortune caused by the action of the Government, first forcing them into this condition, and then forcing them out of it at a time when they are not prepared, and when the market is in such a state as almost to put them in a condition of bankruptcy, if this policy be persisted in.

In another point of view, the discrimination between those who import from foreign countries and those who manufacture at home, must be considered by the Senate. Those who import foreign productions are entitled to three years' time previous to the withdrawal from warehouse of the article that they import. This is in my mind a measure that has not received the consideration, based upon information from the correct source, that it ought to receive. It ought not to pass this body. This constant legislation, affecting existing interests, by Senators who can not be and are not conversant with the interests of this particular subject, is unfortunate. How can they be conversant with it? What I complain of, here and elsewhere, is this constant tampering with the interests in which the people are engaged, in order to force from them Government revenue. The whole legislation here is to protect the Government; and there is, in my deliberate judgment, very little attention paid toward protecting the interests in which the people are engaged.

MR. SHERMAN: I do not want to interrupt my friend, but I desire to say to him that there is not a single clause or section of this bill which is not demanded by persons engaged in the business themselves. Every section of this bill is for their relief, not for the relief of the Government.

MR. SPRAGUE: Complaints come to me from those engaged in this interest. They have satisfied my mind with the correctness of the statements they have made, though they have not apparently affected the mind of the Senator from Ohio.

Mr. President, the attendance to-day is significant. Whether the crowd in the galleries are here from curiosity or from a deep interest in the present condition of the country, each one that occupies these seats can better judge. If they feel as do those who communicate with me on paper, and express themselves concerning the present condition in which this country is, as regards the action of the Government on the interests of the people, they are not here from curiosity, but from a deep anxiety concerning the welfare of the country.

It was observed by my friend, the Senator from Nevada, some time since, that I had united in the measures which had prevailed in Congress. I did not think then to state, as I now do, that it is not only right, but the duty of every man, whether he occupies a private or a public station, when new light breaks in upon him, or when the information and reflections that crowd upon him are of such weight as force him to a different conclusion from that he has heretofore held, to at once change his ground and act according to his honest convictions. I came into this chamber some time ago, from a deep sense of duty, to communicate to the Senate and to the country my reflections on the state of affairs, and the great anxiety that was a second nature to me, that had become a part of my being. It is the policy and practice of the Supreme Court of the United States, notwithstanding there is new light on an old subject, to give to the new subject with new light the decision that it gave to the old subject with the old light. It is for the purpose of maintaining their prestige, regardless of the merits of the case. That is the policy and the practice of all interests that design to perpetuate themselves and to increase their power. There is no other reason why Senators should hold to the opinions that they have heretofore held, except it is to be consistent, strong, arrogating to themselves and to the body power, without regard to the change of circumstances and conditions around them.

Have the people of the United States observed, have reflecting Senators and members of Congress observed, have politicians observed, that there is in our form and system, as now practiced, no check whatever in any of the branches of the Government, or among any of the privileged interests of the people? As to the Executive, what has been the spectacle that has exhibited itself to the country? Was there not an effort that convulsed the country, and blanched the faces of thoughtful men, to bring the President of the United States to the bar of the Senate, to be checked for what the Senate thought was an arbitrary grasp of power? What is the spectacle that has been presented to the country in the last few weeks? The Senate have held on to power with a tenacity equaled only by the hold on power of uncontrolled and unchecked tyranny in the past. I referred a moment ago to the judiciary, in the appointment of which this body shares. Certainly, on a consideration of these three branches of the Government by thoughtful men, they must decide that the powers now exercised by the Senate, in connection with all these three branches of the Government, are far in advance of those that were exercised by them when the Constitution was first established.

We find, too, in the country two great religious bodies arrogating to themselves not only the powers of their holy calling, but exercising an almost controlling power in the political affairs of the country, as well as upon the social condition of the people. I will not point to those who lead in directing the interests of either one or the other of those great institutions; but I point the attention of the reflective mind to their growth and influence otherwise than was originally contemplated, or desirable, when this people first established for themselves a republican form of government.

We had before the Senate, the other day, the spectacle of a contest between two great monopolies. The great railroads across the continent have been here at the bar of the Senate, to contest their claims to an aggregation of more power than they would otherwise have. I point to those great monopolies, and I ask the people of this country if it is a pleasing spectacle to them to find Senators of the United States concerned, on the one side or the other, in advocating the claims of each?

I point to the trades of the country. Is it a pleasing spectacle to witness in the great city of New-York the growth of one or two great interests, and the poverty of all the rest? And when I speak of poverty, those of whom I speak will respond to the words I utter. I point also to the great manufactures, greater now, far greater, than when I first came into the arena of private or public life. I ask the people about and around those great interests whether or not they prefer the present condition of things to the condition in times past, when there were other smaller interests, but who had power as well, and who neutralized and checked the growing and overshadowing influences of the great concerns ?

The example of the Government in arrogating to itself superior powers is followed by the people; and I shall show before I take my seat, that it is owing to a condition of things growing out of the construction of the Government itself.

Sir, I have aroused the attention of the country to their affairs. That must be patent to every Senator. I have not spoken words that have not been spoken at other times, but they did not then touch the popular heart; and why? The popular heart and the popular mind was never before in its present condition, for the reason that the future never looked so dark to the people of the United States as it looks to-day. They do not know what the difficulty is, or how to remedy it. They do know that there is a pressure upon them that they can not throw off. They look to Congress, who have absorbed the powers that I have enumerated, to give them relief; and when they hear words different from the words that have heretofore been uttered, those words command the public attention.

Another reason is that the people know from those utterances that I am conversant with their condition; that I know the causes that have produced that condition; and they feel, from the foreshadowing of the idea of the remedy, that there is hope for them.

I have not come before the Senate or the country for any idle display, or for any purpose of sensation. I certainly do not desire to be the object of the gaze of the people of the United States. I would have preferred to leave this country and to take myself far from the sight and far from the hearing of that which I believe to be, know to be, its ruin, unless there is a reversal of the policy and the acts of this body. I am convinced of it because the facts themselves have impressed it upon me, and because the condition of the people of this country now presents to me an exact parallel to the condition of other people when they commenced their downfall.

The Senate of the United States may well have misunderstood me. It has always been my nature to hide myself from the public gaze. It was my boyish nature. If I was to be found in earlier times, it was easy to find me removed from the confusion and from the observation of all, devoted to my own reflection upon the subjects that were presented to me at the time. Such, sir, is my nature; and there must have been a strong power that could have forced me to the expression of my views and reflections, so contrary to the general sentiment of the body, so at variance with the party now carrying on the affairs of the country. Were I to consult my own convenience and pleasure alone, I would continue, as I had done, silent and apparently inattentive to the business and affairs going on about me. But, sir, I could not do it. I could not resist the pressure that compelled me to speak that which I thought, that which I knew to be the truth, and that which, if not ultimately acted upon, would carry the country to ruin and servitude as certainly as things went on.

I do not speak from feelings or opinions formed now for the first. For some time I have noticed the general tendency of things. If I needed any confirmation of my views, I have it in the fact that the condition of the masses of the people to-day is far more unsatisfactory than it was a year ago. From the South and from all parts of this country come to me letters asking for employment. I am supposed to be rich, and I am made the objective point for these solicitations, perhaps, more than the friends around me. The inquiries that I make and the information that they give confirm me in my opinions, if I needed confirmation.

One great difficulty that exists is that those who possess large interests come here with their attorneys, men familiar with the legal mind, and their case is presented in a legal way, and meets the judgment of the legal mind. The business man, familiar simply with the routine of his own business, not looking much beyond it from day to day, brings to bear upon his interests no language, no information, that can draw the attention of minds thus constituted. It is for that reason that the great business interests of this country, without which the Government is of no avail and the object of its establishment is a failure, suffer.

I think I shall prove conclusively to the minds of all who read that the condition of the country to-day has a parallel in the history of Spain under Philip II. when she lost her possessions and commenced her downward career. I shall point to the Netherlands as another parallel, showing that by the adoption of the plan shadowed forth by me she maintained that supremacy which was the wonder and the astonishment of the world.

Before entering upon my proof, I design—as I have heretofore omitted to mention it among the great powers now absorbing all the interests and all the privileges of the people—to speak of the press. I have a word to say to the press. You are a great power in the land; greater than all the press in other lands combined. With this great power in your hands, one notices that you have not, considering the condition of the country, used it to promote the prosperity of the people. You are represented here by your reporters and correspondents. I speak directly to you both. You pretend to give wholesome advice and right direction to the thoughts of the people. I believe you assume to be the champion of liberty. Freedom of the press is said to be the synonym of freedom for the people. Of course you are always thus engaged. No influence otherwise affects you. In fact, you can not be bribed into the special interest of any body! The young men about me, acting as your correspondents, who find it difficult to live on the pittances doled out to them, are never tempted, of course, by the great corrupting influences around them, into words contrary to the justice and good of the people! If the people come ever to believe the contrary of this—that you are the ready tool of the oppressors of the people, that your watchwords are but a delusion and a snare—your influence will be less than now. But let that go. If you are truthful and do stand truly by the liberties of the people, and war on servitude, why, slur my utterances; why underrate the person who utters them, his arguments, his facts, and his position? If you are true, let us understand it. If you are the tool of the rings, of jobbers, of the great monopolists of the state, of the bar, o the land, or of money, let us understand that also; and the people, who are not yet, I hope, so far reduced as to be incapable of striking a blow in defense of their liberties, will know exactly where to point their guns.

Let it be understood, once for all, that I will not run a newspaper merely, or organize a political party. I am going to advocate a true system of finance based on the great principle which has presented itself to me—the power of the people exercised directly in their own interest. For myself, I enjoy all I can aspire to; I will not be drawn from a great idea, and one which, in my confident belief, will give to my countrymen a higher and nobler position than has ever been enjoyed or even aspired to by any other people since the world began. If, however, I were President of the United States, which is the only office that is the direct representative of all the people, I should make an effort to administer the office based on the general interest and average opinion of the people. To accomplish this, I should throw out from a semi-official source a glimpse of measures that were to be acted upon, as Lincoln did, that there might come to me the views of all conditions of people. It is true safety thus to call up the general judgment; and subjects of public consideration might, by this arrangement, become so modified as practically not to be those originally proposed, and a disclaimer could not be impeached.

We are carrying on this Government now, not only from the lawyer stand-point, but from that of one set of political opinions. There is no safety either to those who enforce the adoption of such opinions or to the people for whom they are enforced. And it is the part of wisdom to oppose them by all the force of reason and logic, presented in a public way, so that neither Radical, Democrat, nor Republican, nor Conservative, or what not, shall have the whole destinies of the people regulated by their theories or views. This is the true place for the President, and it is also the best security for the people. Sir, it is in this as in regulating the money matters of the country. If the Government is carried on by hoarded and centralized opinions, our money affairs may also be as securely carried on by a condition of hoarded and centralized capital. The latter I am at war with. I hope the Administration will consider the suggestions I have here thrown out.

I have repeatedly said that the remedy for our financial difficulties is clear to me, and that it is also sustained by the clearest proofs. Two classes of minds are to be operated upon. Now, the professional mind is affected by a presentation of views only when conclusive to it. The professional man's opinions are modified or sustained or changed altogether by the enforcing on his conviction that form of truth which may enable him to draw just conclusions. We would fail by the introduction of any other character of influence than that to which he is most accustomed. I have many times succeeded in dislodging long-settled ideas and views by antagonizing with them stronger, or those which appeared to be more practical. The professional mind must feel the force of this use of opinion, logic, and reason to influence the logic, opinions, and reason of others. These are practically hoarded and centralized conditions of human thought upon which we seek to operate. I do not use the thumbscrew in removing opinions at variance with mine. I simply desire to marshal thought against thought, that the stronger may triumph. Thus, as mind must meet mind to dissipate ignorance and error, so money must meet money to dissipate capital so injurious at this time to the popular welfare. I would wish that as mind must contend with mind, in the same manner money must dissipate the hoarded and centralized conditions of the money market. It seems to me that I must succeed in establishing my point with professional men by introducing new light into their reflections.

Now, as to the unprofessional mind, the business mind. When the merchant or manufacturer observes capital in a few hands, and out of his reach, he feels its disastrous effects on his trade and business. If he bids more for it than his neighbor, he gets it. He must go into the market as to an auction. Now, he knows that the better condition would be that it should come to him. It can not go to him, however, while in the condition of an auctioneer's sale, because it has formed that business relation. He must be made to see how it can be freed from that relationship. Certainly, if there was in the general money market as great volume or breadth of capital as is now held in few places, and out of his reach, his condition would be very different. The power of centralized, hoarded capital would be equal all around him. If he was pressed on one side by its influence, he would be sustained by a counteracting pressure on the other. A power that will produce that condition is what he seeks. Having it clearly in my own mind, let me see if I can demonstrate it to his. When I draw from the hoarded or centralized capital a part of itself into another equally centralized position—as from banks and bankers, and other capitalists, into the Treasury—which I really propose to do by force of the large sums I would loan out derived from the gold already in the Treasury, by the issue of coin notes thereon, together with the daily balances there, and the Government revenues and individual and other deposits, which deposits are consequent upon the loans, inasmuch as the proceeds of such loans would be replaced in the Treasury, subject only to the ordinary calls of the depositors. Thus, as contemplated by my bill, I should take away from one and give to the other, and if by an arbitrary rule I give it out on the general market from the Treasury into which it had been drawn—and I repeat this process every day—have I not produced an equal condition of the market? Have I not forced the capital of banks, bankers, and capitalists down to a level by the money pressure about them? Can they sponge up the stream from the Treasury as fast as it flows? Certainly not in their weakened state. It seems to me that the intelligence of the business mind must at once perceive the soundness and strength of my position. The lesser must give way to the greater, as is practically effected in all countries where a low rate of interest prevails.

The mass of the people must see that in doing away with the great capitalists under whose manipulations their labor is so unprofitably employed, and substituting therefore a general and equal pressure of money, of which energetic and active men may avail themselves, their condition is substantially improved by labor receiving its fair reward.

I think I shall convince the minds of the masses of the people. I think I shall convince them of the fruitlessness of striking at that which, though now an enemy, may, by the measure I propose, become a friend. The general views and opinions touching currency being based upon the present ruinous condition of things, can not be relied upon as a refuge from the evils felt by the people.

The people must not be deceived by false arguments as to the danger attending the loaning of the public money, or care of the deposits received from the people. Are not the great banks now controlled by one or a few men unchecked? Is not the people's money speculated upon and loaned by hundreds of irresponsible persons—officials of the Government? Is there any watch on their money except the watch with which a boy in the Treasury is charged? That is all. In every government the exercise of this supervision is in the hands of the highest and best men of the nation. This is not so with us. When objection is made relative to this supposed danger, ask them if you have not clothed the Congress with powers, the judiciary with powers, and the Executive with powers; all of which seem to be exercised in the interest of each branch of the Government for itself? The Executive is interested for his class; the Congress for the politicians; the judiciary for the bar. Now, shall not the people have the council of finance in their interest?

It will surprise the American people to know, and it may also be received with a smile when they are for the first time told, that the framers of the Constitution failed to ingraft upon it that which gives life, vitality, and perpetuity to a republican government. They gave us—intentionally or otherwise, I know not—the shadow and excluded the substance. The provincial government and also the union of the States of the Netherlands two hundred and sixty years ago, in other forms, gave far greater liberty to the citizens than ours of to-day. It also better preserved him in the possession of his property. The original settlers of New-York and part of New-England were from those provinces. They were religious people. They established, or thought they did, freedom of conscience; for it was for this that they fled from their homes. They were not familiar with the great principle that underlies society, and without the application of which the personal liberty of the individual in the construction of the state in such only in name. In the study of the history of those states it will be found that that principle is measurably disguised; but it pervades the whole system of government, and gives character and direction to it. It is, as it were, a rudder to a ship—the most insignificant part of a ship in appearance, but it has a power indescribable, and only perceived when it is applied. It was a principle like this that gave to Holland, two hundred and sixty years ago, sixty bushels of wheat to the acre, while we obtain but from five to twelve; and which sent three hundred thousand tons of fish per annum to foreign markets; whose manufactures were sent to every clime; whose harbors were almost inaccessible, and yet whose commerce was larger than that of all Europe besides; and whose territory—little more than one half as large as the State of Rhode Island—sustained in constant employment three millions of people, and held possessions in America and India, the latter of which she holds at this day. She so remained without check until 1694, when the principle on which her prosperity was based was applied by the English people.

I say this principle pervades every phase of the construction of the Government of the provinces and the republic, and was the source from whence came all of our forms of government. The framers of the Constitution of the United States exhibited, in my judgment, a want of practical knowledge and real penetration when they failed to make that principle the most prominent article of our Constitution.

Let us call it a discovery; for no writer on finance, no speculator or philosopher on the action of money, concentrated toward a given point and assaulting the enemy's capital, has shown its results both on property and people. I have said that the principle I speak of was measurably disguised. I quote from the history of those times:

> "We ask why the conduct of the Bank, [of Amsterdam,] instead of being made public, is kept secret and remains mysterious? The true answer is, that should the proprietors of the treasure lodged in the Bank of Amsterdam come once certainly to know that any use was made of the money there deposited, many of them would be apt to think they might as well employ it in the same manner themselves."

These words indicate exactly wherein was concentrated means through which and on which the great prosperity of that nation went on, and the republican form of government maintained.

I say that in my judgment this, though an apology for the framers of the Constitution, goes but little way when from the forms borrowed from the Netherlands the real substance, that which gave these forms value, the council of finance and the loaning of the public money, was neglected and omitted. The truth is, we have been going on from the beginning of our course on a carriage with but three wheels, which ought to have had four. The omission has brought us to our present demoralized and dangerous financial situation. This omission permitted the creation of two great interests for mutual destruction; it caused the loss of the strength of our best lands, kept our manufactures stunted, almost destroyed our commerce—which once destroyed, can never restore itself.

The absence of the financial department of our Government is best exhibited by an account of the council of finance in Burrish's "Batavia Illustrata," concerning the different branches of that republic called the republic of the Netherlands:

"Section IV.

"Of the Council of State and General Chamber of Accompts.

"The erection of the Council of State was projected by the States of Holland, Zealand, and Utrecht in concert with that great politician William I., Prince of Orange. The tragical and unexpected death of this prince, contrary to all expectation, produced very little alteration in the measures that had been taken in his lifetime for the establishment of this council, which the States General erected in the same year, 1584, with a very ample authority. Affairs of state, both foreign and domestic, the army and revenue, were all intrusted to her care; but the States themselves soon grew jealous of this extraordinary power, which they resolved to reduce gradually; and accordingly by a new instruction, in 1651, the disposition of military affairs and the command of the army, from being peculiar to the council, was in part transferred to the States General, who now give orders for the safety and defense of the State, the motion of the troops, and the operations of the campaign. But this is not done without consulting the council, however, which still retains the care of raising and disbanding, clothing and arming the soldiers, of exercises and reviews, and in general of all the military discipline and economy. She is likewise charged with the care of the fortifications and magazines of Gelderland and Overyssel, which make the frontier of the seven provinces.

"Business of state, especially that which is foreign, depends now entirely on the States General; but the council still retains the inspection of the general revenue of the union, and gives orders for payments; on which account the treasurer general has his seat at this board, and a right to debate, but not to vote. The office of treasurer is for life, which gives him an opportunity of acquiring so perfect a knowledge of affairs as makes him entirely necessary. It is he who prepares every year, under the authority of the council, an exact account of the funds necessary for maintaining the troops and officers in pay, and all other expenses that regard the generality; which is what they call *l'Etat de la Guerre.*

"The receiver-general attends here likewise, to instruct the council what funds are in his hands; which being done, he withdraws. The treaty of union obliges each province to levy certain taxes, to be applied to the common necessities of the whole body; but this article could never be executed and probably never will, because the inland provinces, who have little or no commerce, can not possibly pay an equal quota with those where trade flourishes. The following proposition is what each province always pays in the sum of one hundred gilders or florins.

* * * * * * *

"They do not always confine themselves, however, within their settled proportions, but raise such sums and by such ways and means as they think proper, of which they send their quota to the receiver-general, and employ the rest as they please. In time of war, when the ordinary revenues are not sufficient for the necessary expense, the council demands the settlement of new funds from the States General; and to these extraordinary expenses the provinces contribute in the following proportion.

*   *   *   *   *   *   *   *

"In the assemblies of the States General and provincial States the suffrages are not taken *capiatim*, but *provincialiter;* and therefore the provinces and the towns may send what number of deputies they please, because they all virtually have but one voice. But in this council the provinces are represented by such a number of deputies as bears a tolerable proportion to the money which each of them contributes for the support of the whole, with exception only to Groningen. Gelderland has one, Holland three, Zealand two, Utrecht one, Friesland two, Overyssel one, and Groningen two, who, with the deputies of the nobles and governors of the provinces, are the persons that compose the Council of State. And here each member has a decisive voice, and presides in his turn, without regard to the rank of the provinces.

"For the regulation of accompts between the provinces, and auditing those of particular receivers; with the income of the lands which belong to the state in general, there is a chamber of accompts, composed of fourteen deputies of all the provinces, and two secretaries, who likewise do the business of auditors and correctors. This chamber examines the accompts of the several admiralties, who receive the money arising from duties of importation and exportation, appropriated by the States to the service of the navy. In the same manner she superintends and regulates the expenses of the States deputies who travel and execute commissions for the public; the salaries and extraordinary expenses of ambassadors, extraordinary deputies, and other ministers employed in foreign courts; and keeps an exact register of all orders made by the Council of State, for whose ease she was indeed chiefly erected."

Thus, sir, is seen in the construction of that Government a power equal almost to the executive power, that superintended all he money received and all the money paid out by the Government. As with us judges are appointed for life that they may be familiar with the law and with the precedents, so as to give uniform and correct judgments in cases that are brought before them by the people; so here we find that that important branch of the government, the charge of the finances, was placed in the same relation to that interest that the judicial branch of our Government holds to the bar. These men who occupied the position of Council of State were men exalted in name, in character, and in ability, beyond those about them. When, as I have observed, all the funds that were inspected by this great power were centralized and used in the interest of the people, regulating their business, controlling all their great departments of state, and giving to that people a prestige never attained by a similar number of people in the world, I must certainly draw the attention of the people of the country to the omission that I have referred to in the formation of our Government: the omission of a financial department to correct the growing arrogance and power of other branches of the Government, and to correct and check the overshadowing powers that are growing up and destroying the interests of the people.

In connection with this subject we should consider the situation of the three million people who have built their habitations almost upon the sea. In a paragraph in the same history we are told that

> "The large dikes or ramparts, which they throw up to keep out the water, are an immoderate expense to the country; and what is still worse, the sea and the ice very often cut and break through their strongest works, or force over them in such a manner that it often takes up years to free the country from the inundation, and restore it to its former circumstances.
>
> *   *   *   *   *   *   *   *
>
> "But this situation, however inconvenient and unpleasant, has its advantages with relation to commerce; for there being very little land in Holland, and that extremely bad, the merchant has no temptation to draw his money out of trade; which continues to accumulate, from one generation to another, and by this means becomes so plenty, and interest so very low, that the Dutch are from thence, in a great measure, enabled to sell cheaper than their neighbors."

Here is conclusively shown that, by the operation of the council of finance and the introduction of the government money upon the market, there was obtained a low rate of interest, by means of which and through which a population of three millions obtained their livelihood, and sustained a commerce greater than that of all the world beside.

These three million people were thus employed, according to this authority: five hundred thousand in the sea fisheries, including those who built the vessels and supplied them with necessaries; two hundred and fifty thousand in the agriculture of the country; eight hundred thousand in manufactures; three hundred thousand in building, equipping, and navigating all kinds of ships and trading vessels; eight hundred thousand in procuring and furnishing all things necessary for the support of life, aliments of all sorts, with clothes, buildings, furniture, and all the long train of conveniences, superfluities, and embellishments; and the remaining three hundred and fifty thousand were the nobility; those in employments, lawyers, all those that lived on their rents, with their servants, the military men, and the poor.

This was the condition of the people whose commerce was maintained in the supremacy I have indicated. I ask the people of this country to examine into the present condition of their foreign commerce, and to ask themselves if it does not conclusively show that they fail in having that element of strength that this prosperous and powerful republic, of two hundred and sixty years ago, possessed.

I again quote from the same authority in reference to the manufactures of the various provinces:

"To this prodigious extent of foreign commerce we must add the manufactures ascribed to the several towns above mentioned; all of which, with exception only to the Delft-ware, are more or less practiced in this powerful and opulent city."

Referring to Amsterdam:

"A multitude of hands are employed in all kinds of tapestry. There are numbers of mills for sawing all sorts of wood into different dimensions. Others to work and polish marble; mills for making gunpowder, for grinding snuff, and for drawing oil from seed. There are refineries for sugar, salt, cinnamon, camphor, borax, sulphur, yellow wax, etc. And, as Huetius observes, one may apply to Amsterdam what Vopiscus said of Alexandria, after he had summed up the manufactures practiced there: 'That all its inhabitants followed some trade; that the lame and the gouty were employed, and even those who had the gout in their hands did not sit idle.'"

Now, sir, I have presented as well as I could the simple condition which gave to the republic from which we obtained our form of government the prosperity that she enjoyed. I have given it from a history written at a period familiar with that situation, and there can not be any mistake in reference to it. Let me next refer to the condition in which Spain found herself when by the efforts of Charles V. she ruled most of Europe, and lost it. If she did not rule it by possession of territory, she yet ruled it politically and commanded the situation. When I draw attention to the causes and the circumstances attending the downfall of the Spanish monarchy, the people of the United States will see conclusively the influences that are contributing to the downfall of this country. I read from the same authority to which I have already referred:

"Every body knows that the force and grandeur of Spain depends on the annual returns that she receives from her colonies in the West-Indies; and were the treasures that are brought from those countries to remain entirely with the Spaniards they would be more than sufficient to render them what they once were, the most redoubtable enemies and most tyrannical allies in the universe. But the incapacity of Spain to furnish a cargo for the supply of the West-Indies forces her to share the profits of that commerce with the other trading nations of Europe, and thus the return of the galleons and the flotilla is as necessary to the merchants of France, England, and Holland as to those of Cadiz and Madrid.

"This poverty which incapacitated the Spanish to supply the West-Indies arises from mismanagement in their European commerce. The vast equipments made by Philip II., and the ill-success of his enterprises, had so totally destroyed the naval power of Spain that after the peace of Munster the Spaniards found themselves obliged to hire Dutch vessels to carry on their trade to America. The wars they were afterwards engaged in with France, the sums expended in the preservation of the Netherlands, as well as the Italian States dependent on the Crown of Spain, the vast numbers of men consumed in the defense of those countries, from the peace of Munster to the death of Charles II., and the several calamities which harassed Spain from the decease of this prince to the peace of Utrecht, have been so many invincible impediments to the revival of their navigation. Since the treaty of Utrecht they have been zealous to restore their maritime force, but have been mistaken in the means.

"If the money laid out by the Court of Madrid in the Sicilian expedition and the equipment of that fleet, which was so entirely defeated by our admiral, my Lord Torrington, in 1718, had been employed for the immediate encouragement of navigation either in the nature of loans to particular merchants or any other effectual method for fitting out merchant ships in the several ports of Spain, I believe that by this time the Spaniards would have been able to carry on their European commerce entirely with their own ships, and this would in a little time enable them to fit out a navy and to supply their West-Indies without the assistance of any foreign nation. But the Spanish Court was resolved to have a fleet at any price, before they had laid the necessary foundation for its support—that is, before they had extended their own navigation so as to have a constant nursery for seamen, and before they had a sufficient quantity of stores in their country to repair any sudden loss, without which it is vain to think of keeping up a navy, except at such an expense as even all the treasures of the Indies would not be equal to."

Philip II. would have a navy at any price; and instead of strengthening his people through their industries, he drew from them revenues sufficient to build his navy, by which means his commerce was destroyed. Is there not a parallel between his course and the policy of Congress, and those who are influencing congressional action, in enforcing specie payments upon the nation regardless of every interest in which the people are engaged? If there is any application in the words quoted, and in the circumstances attending the forcing upon the Spanish people of the building of a navy, do they not warn us as to the consequences of forcing upon this people a condition of specie payments by which and through which their industries are to be prostrated; for is it not evident to the mind of every man that by law, as by any other system of speculation, there has been brought into the money market a force, backed by the whole power of the Government, which has resulted in the increased price of money from the beginning of that experiment until the present time?

Sir, there is no industrial interest in this country that can obtain a profit to-day based upon the interest that the Government itself has elected to pay by the forcing of capital into the hands of the few and out of the hands of the many. If reflecting men can not and will not see in this the cause of the destruction of their interests and the precarious condition of their affairs, and the wrong policy that has been pursued here from the beginning, they must be blind indeed. Philip II. forced his people to build him ships to carry on his wars. He took from them the very means that would have sustained his commerce and his manufactures. And what have we done but to take the means of the people from their industries to establish by force a condition of specie payments, and give an increased value to government securities? The Congress of the United States are to-day managing not only the political condition of the people, but they are certainly managing every individual and every collective interest of the United States. There is not an interest that there is not a constant agitation for some law respecting it. No business-man knows to-day what Congress may do to-morrow, what laws they may enact, and no man knows how to provide to-day for a year from now, not knowing what will be done in Congress. Sir, is that the business that men who occupy seats here should devote themselves to? Why not let the people alone in the management of their affairs? Why draw from them that which alone can give vigor, strength, and activity to their operations?

I have, Mr. President, felt called upon to criticise in the best language that I possess those matters which were deemed by me to be imperfect. I have endeavored to show to the people of the country, and to turn the attention of Senators, by truthful utterances, toward the exact condition of matters here and elsewhere. I am certainly confirmed in the position I have taken by the indications that come to me from all quarters. I can not hesitate to characterize strongly the growing, monopolizing, and vicious powers that are coming unchecked upon the people; and I deem it a duty to bring to bear upon that condition of things such illustrations, and point to those which to me are most applicable.

I have pointed to the action of Congress, members of the two Houses, in the demands they make upon the attention of the executive department for office; but I have not pointed to a condition of things among the people that is as vicious, that is as injurious to communities, to states, and to nations, as the operations of the members of Congress in applications for prerogatives and offices for their friends.

As I said, I use the best illustration at command to show the pernicious influence of those who control capital merely on legislation, society, business, and even on the fortunes of war. Any reflecting mind may easily perceive that the people are made both cowardly and poor by such influences, exercised as they now are and heretofore have been. It has been said, and I have had a powerful experience to support the truth of the saying, that there is nothing at once so cowardly and so vicious as five hundred thousand dollars, except—a million.

Now for my illustration:

There is in my State a great capital centred in one family; and that family has a newspaper organ, and that newspaper organ is controlled by my colleague. There are throughout the State those who receive or expect to receive stipends at the hands of that family, or whose business rests on its favors.

They and their agents are in possession of most of the moneyed institutions of the State, and when they sneeze, there is a great deal of sneezing from one end of the State to another. No man knows, unless he conducts a large business, how sensitive credit is in times of stringency in the money market. It is like the virtue of a woman, easy to be stabbed in secret. The slander gathers strength as it goes, and the character has suffered a wound from which it never recovers. But the cowardly attack, of course, indicates a cowardly nature.

It will be remembered that I commented a few days ago on a paragraph which had recently appeared in my colleague's newspaper. I desire to say to the people of Rhode Island and the country that those who hold in their hands large masses of the capital of a community influence the course which all the capital of that community takes, no matter how situated. If the holders of such capital are moved by envy or hostility, they have it in their power to sacrifice those who by the exercise of their own energies are carrying on extensive operations. I ask the people of Rhode Island if it would please them to see the great interests I represent receive the stab I have described? But the effort to stab me has at least been made. The members of the great moneyed family I have adverted to have taken recent occasion to say to those controlling capital heretofore employed by me, that "SPRAGUE is very much extended," "SPRAGUE is investing in the South," "SPRAGUE is doing a very great business;" and all this with a shake of the head which shook the heads of all around, as much as to say that they did not know how it would come out. I struck back, direct at the hand which struck the blow, and which, after striking, wrote an account of it for my colleague's paper. I took occasion to state the reason for using the credit these vicious eyes called attention to. It was that I was carrying large stocks at fifty to seventy-five per cent less than others were doing. The effect of this was to keep the New-England mills in operation. Suppose the market for these cloths was allowed to drift down to seven cents per yard, how long would the mills have been kept running with cotton at thirty-two cents per pound? And if the general market had been met and lowered instead of held up, how long would those who used those goods at even so low a figure as seven cents a yard be able to keep them in the general market? When they know that six hundred thousand pieces, in different forms, but in one mass, of these cloths were held out of the market by the use of the credit sought to be damaged, what will they say? What was the satisfaction of those who—others than those I represent—when it was no longer possible to hold up the market, were driven by their necessities to accept less prices than the market price, when the whole volume of goods were sold following their action, held up by the means I have indicated? When the New-England manufacturers can see an inch before their eyes, they will see that the whole policy of those I represent has ever been to enable those about them to go on and profit in their business enterprises. I challenge the first instance to the contrary. Without this policy the labor employed in the various manufactories about us would have received far less reward than it did receive. Those I aim at long ago scented the idea that when great credit or great capital is used to sustain or depress the market the object is usually effected. I disparage these great business concerns; but, sir, the inevitable tendency of things is to them. Let my people remember that not many years ago there were numerous small interests about me where there is not one now. All are consolidated; and these consolidations work serious injury to the independent character of the laboring people. Great interests must war on smaller ones in order to sustain themselves. It is the inevitable consequence of the imperfect character of our legislation and Government. Riches find their way to the pockets of the rich, and deeper poverty comes to the homes of the poor. If I can help it, I will not live among a people who are paupers, and who bid fair to become slaves to these great institutions.

This is my war. It is not a war upon them; but it is a war to give to the people equal facilities with these great establishments, that they may safely employ their energies in the same business, and of course as competitors with them, and as checks upon their power and supremacy.

I will not have a whole community subject to a bad condition of my stomach, or subject to all the ills humanity is heir to. What is that but an abnormal condition among the people? Am I warring against my own interests? Will a people who are made poor by the operations of these powerful establishments among them permit the inequality of great poverty for themselves; great riches in the hands of the few? Not unless they are slaves, sir. So far I am not at war with my own interests, as those about me, without this statement of facts, might be induced to believe. I have taken my position because I believe I see further and clearer than the holders of the power I have indicated. They are like the stragglers who, when the line is presented in full front to the enemy, are in greater danger than those who are receiving the full fire of the opposing forces. I have heard that there are more stragglers—those who fall out of line or who crowd together—killed than among the courageous and faithful who stand unswerved in correct alignment, receiving the fire of the enemy, and doing good execution against them.

I proceed with my illustration. This great family came to me in 1857, and made this proposition: "Let us join our forces, prevent a suspension of specie payment, break down those who are our rivals in business, or otherwise, and buy up their property." At that time I had no debts whatever pressing upon me. But did I unite with them in carrying into effect this vicious and pernicious scheme? Sir, I did not. I repudiated and spurned the proposal, as I now do the proposition to continue the present state of our affairs, which is really to my temporary advantage.

But what, I ask the people of Rhode Island, was the character of the enterprise of this great family? Have they not from the beginning of their history sent out of the State all the capital upon which they could lay their hands? When shamed into the fashion of employing some of their immense resources in the business of the people about them, did they not set an example, in the extravagance of their buildings, which others of less ability were induced to follow, almost or altogether to their ruin? And have they not conducted their business in such ignorant and unskillful manner as to cause injury to nearly every one engaged in business near them? Such at least, sir, is my experience; for I have enterprises in the poisonous atmosphere they create. The people must know that they are directly injured by those who are ignorant and unskillful in the management of their own affairs. Their interests are the people's interests, and the sooner those who are the custodians of them come to this belief, the better for all.

So much for business. I proceed still further with my illustration.

The great family I have mentioned are influential in the management of our college, the venerable Brown University. This institution has nothing in sympathy with the people of Rhode Island. Do the people know that it is because the business office of the great power managed it out of the State? Do they know that they drove from the office of president the intellectual seers who would not submit to the vicious power that would either rule or ruin? Do they know that the Western lands given to the State for an agricultural college, and given to the university through my action—worth now more than a million dollars, if the Senator from Kansas [Mr. POMEROY] be a good witness—were sold for $50,000, and bought by an agent of the college, who aided in procuring funds for the college, and who is the "right bower" of the great power I have described? And, in short, do the people know that the feud this power has engendered keeps the college in turmoil and confusion, a disgrace to the noble work it was intended it should perform? Are such great establishments any especial advantage to the community, in an educational point of view?

Mind, Mr. President, I use this as an example to illustrate just how the people of this country are controlled and driven to their ruin. The instance is only one of many, but perhaps an aggravated case, which the imperfections of our institutions give existence to; like that I referred to the other day of ten per cent a month.

In a religious view, it will be my duty hereafter to refer to them. In politics, after a simple statement concerning the Dorr war, I shall confine myself to my personal experience. I speak, sir, of the public action, and the public results of their action. I shall await the action of their instrument before coming to a nearer inspection of that which is private. I say, then, that the great Dorr war, which decided a national election, was brought on the people of the State by their management, and ended under their direction.

Now as to my own knowledge touching their political action. Like the inquisition, they work in the dark. The people do not yet know that they have been led about by the nose by their influence. I will tell them.

It is known that I arrived from Europe in the winter of 1860; that I received an ovation never theretofore given to a private citizen; that at that time what was called the radical wing of the Republican party had nominated their candidate. The candidate was not the tool of the great family. At once there was an uproar, and opposition was organized. I was tempted with a proposition to put me in nomination. I refused, as I had previously pledged myself that I would not enter politics. I was young; I had no political knowledge, and no knowledge of the real hand at work. I was told that it was of national importance that the radical element should be suppressed. I refused for a week; but finally I consented. The Republican party was defeated, and lost power for three years. When I had placed myself in the breach, the great power, with characteristic cowardice, held aloof. This power was that which in this way gave the staggering blows that broke up the party in Rhode Island, and made the struggle to elect Lincoln far greater than it would otherwise have been; for the leaders of the party thought there was a change of opinion among the people, and that such might be the case throughout the country. There was not an atom of principle in their work; there was a greed for power only.

I ask the people of Rhode Island and of the country if such

unscrupulous powers growing up among them are safe to their liberties? I answer a thousand times, No!

I was fated. But did I surrender to further temptation? Let my subsequent action show. I saw the impending war. When it came, I went into the armories and among the people, and organized twelve hundred men, with new officers. But in the regiment the great power exhibited itself. And now comes a most interesting phase of the war. History by my silence shall never be led astray. In this regiment, then, I found the power. It came to Washington. I urged immediate action; I constantly urged a movement on Richmond before the Confederates concentrated there. The movement would have been successful, as all said. The strongest opposition came from the rich men in the regiment. These rich men were the power I am criticising. Remember there is nothing so cowardly as five hundred thousand dollars—except a million. And remember it was heralded all over the country; gratified at the unusual spectacle of rich men willing to expose their lives for their country. I posted one of them to guard the revolutionary flag from an excited officer. Did he stand fire? Sir, he ran away at the first attack upon him; like a coward, deserted his post. He threatened dire vengeance when both himself and the officer returned to private life; but I never heard that there was any account presented or enforced.

Well, we did not move. We remained fêted, flattered, and covered all over with admiration. However, I went home to organize a new regiment for the three years' service. Prior to its coming, the regiment moved with the other forces on Harper's Ferry. I hastened from the State and joined them. The movement resulted in nothing; it was too slow. We moved in fear. Sir, fear prevailed in my regiment. Finally we moved to attack the enemy at Manassas. We were at Centreville. The Secretary of War came up. We were brigaded with other regiments; the Secretary of War admired the command. The commanding general relied upon us more than upon double the same force in the army.

But what was the rumor that came to me? What! the regiment refused to move; their time was out. What was the influence exercised here? Sir, it was the million dollars. Their lives were precious; they were three months' men; the lives of the three years' men were not precious. They were poor mechanics; they were fit only to die; but the million dollars would seek safety in a miserable subterfuge. The Secretary of War came to me; the general commanding the army came to me. "What do we hear? Rhode Island refuses to move. There are ten thousand men awaiting the action of your regiment. We will be forced in disgrace to return."

I sent for the colonel. He said the rumor was true. What was my answer to him? "Go back to your command; say to the rebellious—the million dollars—that the country has exalted them to the skies with its praises; that Rhode Island expects them to fight," and, with some emphatic words not now necessary to repeat, that "they should fight, or I would disgrace them to the State and the country." This quelled the disturbance.

I was at the defeat at Blackburn's Ford. I was in the front of the enemy with the only reconnoissance of line that was made. I was the only man from the State who was in that dangerous service. I wanted to feel the enemy; I wanted myself to see him. I did see him for a whole day with but one hundred regular cavalry, nearer than the million dollars ever came.

But anon the forces moved. We were the light division; we were to march in the rear of the line; we were the flanking force, and in the most danger, because we were considered the most reliable. The three years' men acted part as skirmishers, part as reserve. The artillery came next, then the first regiment with its million dollars in high command, and following the other regiments of the brigade. We crossed Cub Run; we felt the enemy; we came upon him posted not forty paces from us. The gallant Slocum formed line on the left of the road with great intrepidity, under fire; the raw levies stood firm as veterans, delivered their fire with precision, and the battle went on; we had no time to look behind.

I took special charge of the battery. The men, detached and separated, were a little confused; some stood firm. Horses were struck down; men lay down and died; for ten minutes I supplied the gun with cartridges and ammunition to give confidence to the line. I kept my horse during the fight; the bullets scratched me and made holes in my loose blouse.

The brave Ballou came to me. With a harsh expression I ordered him back to his regiment. "Where is Slocum?" "Dead." "Where are so and so?" naming a dozen officers. "Dead." "Go back and keep your men to their work; see that they work together." Ballou said: "I come to get assistance; the enemy are flanking us." "Where are the million dollars?" They can not be found. Nobody was there, and they were going it alone, and for forty minutes stood without assistance. Where were our companions? Echo answers—where? Here are the mechanics, who are good enough to be shot and nothing more.

We directed an organized force on our left; we turned our artillery in that direction. We looked for the million dollars. Did it come? Yes; the commander, in fright and alarm, finally brought them from their security in the woods. How did they come? Sir, they came like a flock of sheep. They formed line like a flock of sheep; they fired in the air. One of the representatives of the million dollars skulked, and his officer disgraced him with a blow of his sword. His reply was that when he got the officer in civil life he would settle the account. But that was the last of it.

Where was he who was placed in high command over this devoted and splendid body of men, whose equal had never before been brought together? for remember it was the vicious influence of only one or two men who were here. Where was he, I say? He had left, had deserted them. He sought safety in safe places. He was not there. The men well remember when I rode in front of them, struck down their muskets to a level with the enemy, and how they received me—the only officer they had whom they could see; and I shall never forget the sensation which I felt in the blast of the enthusiasm with which these twelve hundred men received me. We were ripe then for a charge. I led. Sir, my horse was then shot. I took off his saddle in front of the line; and the men, without order and without energetic pushing, fell back. The enemy continued his fire. I saw the commander of the brigade; I inquired of him, "Where are the officers?" His face was covered with tears; his million dollars should not be sacrificed. With three thousand men unemployed, he harassed McDowell for three hundred regulars to come to his support. They came and cleared the field, and the million dollars was saved.

The regiment was led away; but the artillery remained, and I with it. I inspected the field. I received the full blast of Johnston's reënforcement, not twenty paces off. I saw the men scattered; they were not held to the line.

I returned to the hidden regiments and advised immediate organization to guard the rear; that they should be the rear-guard and hold the post of danger. Did they stand a moment? Sir, the million dollars, had they been in front, where they belonged—four thousand men, three thousand of whom had suffered nothing—would, if pushed, have carried the day. The army knew it. The general commanding knew it, and has so said. I knew it.

Now for the rear-guard. Did they stand? No, sir. The first scattering men that came along scattered them. I made further efforts to organize a guard from among the men coming in. I succeeded for a time; but the haste of the million dollars going to the rear left the space too great, and we dissolved. I gave it up in despair. I joined the million dollars. News came that the enemy were pursuing. With blanched face I was begged bv the commander, who was stupefied by the million dollars, to take a white flag and go to the rear and surrender the troops, as he would not have them cut up. Twice, sir, was I thus solicited. Did I spurn with contempt, or not, the miserable and cowardly proposition? Sir, we were disgraced.

We moved to our camp at Centreville. I was exhausted with the work of the day; for my bodily strength was not great. I sent to the conference of generals the commander of the million dollars, but who, it will be observed, was the real power directing affairs, with the injunction that we stay there; that we fortify our position; that we should not go back like sheep to Washington; that we should not be further disgraced. Sir, what was their action? I went to sleep; and about two o'clock the stillness awoke me. All had fled; had been gone for hours. I saddled my horse, jumped the fences, and reported to Lincoln; and begged him to send forward new troops which he had to stop the disorder. My petition was of no avail.

The million was asked to wait a week. The enemy were coming on. Sir, why not stop in a place of security? Certainly no one would now refuse. A rat will fight in a corner; a coward will sometimes be worked up to a frenzy. Sir, the million dollars would not stay. The very next train put distance between them and their fancied pursuers. Thus the mechanics were sacrificed. They would not have been had the enemy not found all his forces operating on a short line.

One hundred men paid the penalty. They were poor men, however. The battle was lost beyond a peradventure by the influences that kept the forces in the rear. As splendid a body of men as ever shouldered a musket, other than the million dollars, were disgraced. A nation was paled and discouraged; a State hung its head; and only in its mechanics, in the infantry and artillery, had she a decent place in history.

Sir, it was the influence of the million dollars that struck at me.

They went home; paid *claqueurs* were ready, and an ovation followed. The feelings the *claqueurs* gave rise to embarrassed me when I was in the field. A spirit of disorder and disunion was engendered in every regiment the State sent into the front. One was hardly formed before this counter influence was at work. Is this the kind of direction for a brave people? Is this the sort of influence that it is desirable the American people should build up? I say, No; a thousand times no.

How did the country and my colleague and this Senate reward that action? By a commission as brevet brigadier-general!

Besides this, be it understood that there was a solemn oath taken by the million dollars to bare the breast to the bullets of the enemy, and I had taken no such oath. I was but an actor without commission or authority, but did act as I have related.

Did not the power, in subsequent political action, send a man to Congress who has covered the business interests of the State with disgrace?

It is influences of this kind, now at work in every community throughout the country in a greater or less degree, that I propose to reduce to a position where they will cease to rule.

MR. ANTHONY: Will my colleague allow me to ask him to whom he refers?

The VICE-PRESIDENT: Does the Senator from Rhode Island yield to his colleague?

MR. SPRAGUE: No, sir. My colleague says it is painful to him. To me there is no pain when gathering instruction from the past for the guidance of the future. He may say that one of the representatives of the power lost his life. True, sir; the million dollars mistook the character of the man on whose staff he was, and placed a member of the family there who fell with his chief. It made some atonement, but where are the one hundred men dead? How atone for a battle lost, a nation humbled, twelve hundred men for life cut off from the enjoyment of believing that their efforts, if properly and courageously directed, would have saved a nation from humiliation, a State from disgrace, and themselves from bitterness. One life does not always repay for a work of this kind. The life must be a great one. We have heard of such a one, but it does not belong to this account. We gather this moral from this chapter in history—that a people under such control and direction become cowards and slaves; and gather this also, that under any other government on the face of the globe death would have been the penalty, not the highest honors of the state.

Mr. President, I will not burden the Senate describing similar influences that worked disaster to the Army of the Potomac. I will forego that for the present. But I am cautioned to exercise policy; that the adversary must be approached in parallel and zigzag lines. Are the people forced into such danger that they can not approach, but under cover, the institutions built by their consent and sanctioned by their labors?

Following out the illustration of the influences I have described as at work in Rhode Island, let me ask the people of my State how they like the increasing growth of these two great houses—my own and that of the great family I have mentioned? They are now at war; suppose they were to join hands; what independence would there be among a people so largely composed of the manufacturing class? Let us understand the whole case. The condition of affairs in our State, which is but an aggravated one in its application to the whole country, is this, and nothing less. Go back with me to the Middle Ages and see how by personal courage and daring great chiefs sprung up, surrounded themselves with vassals, and intrenched themselves with castles, the ruins of which still interest travelers, though they do not often instruct them. Thus established, baron warred on baron, destroying castles and capturing vassals and lands, and adding them to his own. For a long period leaders and people were occupied in war, and continued so until trade and commerce were established. Is not our situation similar, except that instead of noble daring among the leaders and manly courage and virtue among the people, there are at work those secret influences which make cowards and paupers? Does not the great capitalist destroy and absorb the less, as the great baron destroyed the smaller? And was not the baron who possessed himself by force of the castles, lands, and vassals of another like the great capitalist absorbing to himself the property and business of his weaker competitor? As for me, if I were called which to choose, the condition of the Middle Ages or now, I should choose the former. Then the lands of the people were laid waste by the contending chieftains, and the despoiler aggregated the spoils to himself. Do we not see wasted our lands, our property, our commerce and trade; our business of all kinds absorbed by the great moneyed institutions growing up about us? Will not these great interests war on each other, and whoever triumphs, will not the people, in like manner, suffer and be impoverished? Sir, I certainly think so.

The power of the barons was only checked and destroyed when the barons and people united in the selection of a leader, the better to protect themselves from foreign inroads and from one another. This seems to me significant; but that significance ends when a power at the disposal of the people and the one I indicate is brought into being.

I have illustrated this with a purpose. I have given the history of the influence of money, of the power of money in its operation on the men that influence legislation, society, business, and every thing in this country, with a purpose. It is no easy task for any man to stand up against the overshadowing money-power. I know the essence of money; I know what forces it will bring to bear as well as any man who hears me or who may read what I say. I know that the influence of any one representing simple capital on this Congress, in affecting the legislation of the country, is as certain to be in antagonism to the liberties and interests of the people as in the war instance I have illustrated. I do not desire to point a finger that will in any way destroy them; they are proper and necessary in their place, but when they come here and use this Senate as their agent, and manipulate laws in their interest to control the whole Government of this country and the people's interest, then I denounce it; then I desire, as the people of the country desire, that there shall be an agency at work that will regulate, that will control, that will reduce them to subjection to the people's interests. There can be no mistake in the picture that I have drawn. Senators must stop and consider. They must see that in the influence, in the encouragement they are giving to these overshadowing powers there is danger; and when they further consider the anxieties, and cares, and sufferings, and poverty, that are growing upon the people every day and every hour, it seems to me that it is time for them to pause and consider if the policy they have pursued is the correct policy. I say it is not; the people say it is not. Then, sir, why not pause and consider whether you are right or they?

The governments of England and of the Continent know that your system of finance, or rather your want of a system, has rottenness in it, and that under it you can not go on and pay your debts. The only danger attending the adoption of the plan I propose is that Great Britain and the other Powers, seeing you establish yourselves upon a sound financial bottom, may seek to prevent you. Will they go to war to prevent you? It is not impossible. They have looked with suspicion at your securities; while those of Great Britain bring ninety to ninety-five at three per cent interest, yours at six per cent bring only eighty. They know yours have no real bottom on which to rest; but they will sell to you as long as you have a dollar to pay for their goods. They will take advantage of your poverty so long as your lands sell at half or a quarter of their value. This is going on at a rapid rate; and you see by the increase of importations—indicative of the unemployment of your people in manufactures, produced by the extortionate rates of interest established for your public securities—that the increase in the cost of your manufactures is so great that the tariff is becoming of no possible protection. But you can not increase the tariff, you can not increase the taxes, and operatives are unemployed. There is a less and less market for your agricultural productions. Existing prices are starvation prices, because your people are in great numbers in the position of unemployment. You can not ship it, as you can not compete and pay the transportation with a production on your part of five to twelve bushels to the acre against a production of twenty-seven and twenty-eight; and all you sell at one hundred and forty cents a bushel of wheat here, being equal to a production of seven to ten dollars to the acre, will not pay the labor you put on it; so that your agricultural commerce is already lost. Your manufacturing and mechanical interests are going the same way, as may be seen by the facts I have enumerated. What, I ask, have you to rely on to give credit or to give strength to national or any other of your securities? Of course, while this state of things is going on the world will look on and laugh at you. That they will send back their bonds just in time to save themselves and take more of your capital now in business is a fact, I believe, patent to every body. The vast amount of bonds now in Europe unsold, on which bills of exchange are drawn, gives a fictitious appearance of strength to your market. I repeat, that it may be that when England becomes convinced that your eyes are opened, that you see your real condition and are about to apply an effectual remedy, and that remedy one that will take from her her supremacy of trade with you; that you will through its means establish your republican institutions upon solid foundations, restore your manufactures and your commerce independently of her—at that moment she may allege a pretext for war upon you. But with a substantial financial system fully ingrafted on your political system you can laugh at the world and defy them all. Without a good financial system you are weakness itself. You will take warning, I hope, by my words. I quote some instructive sentences:

> "It is the constant interest of trading nations never to undertake offensive wars for the sake of glory and conquest. They must remain upon the defensive, and not come to an open rupture with their neighbors but upon the utmost necessities.
>
> "This is a settled maxim with all countries that depend upon traffic. But as there is no rule that is not liable to an exception, there are certainly some cases in which it would be the interest of the United Provinces to declare war against Spain, notwithstanding the inconvenience which the republic must suffer from a suspension of her commerce."

Such was the attitude of the Dutch toward Spain. Such may become the attitude of Great Britain toward us.

I look with pleasing anticipations on the results of the measure I advocate. I feel that when it is in complete operation the people will not be compelled again to look to a single man for relief or safety, nor to no party will they surrender their destinies, and to no Congress as a point toward which they must turn their eyes in anxious forebodings. The people will have safety in the strength of their own position. I am confident they will accept my measure, and that they will ultimately protect it as the apple of their eye.

In conclusion, I pray the people of the South to turn from the contemplation of their wrongs, and the people of the North no longer to blame the South as the cause of their sufferings. Let them come to the conviction that the cause of their troubles is in the imperfection of Government. Let them reflect that an important element in the Government, one that would have given it superior strength and vitality, was omitted. Let us set at once to work to remedy the imperfection, and by the help and blessing of God the bitterness engendered by the war may be done away with, and we, as one people, move onward to permanent prosperity and happiness, and to a higher and higher civilization.

www.ingramcontent.com/pod-product-compliance
Lightning Source LLC
LaVergne TN
LVHW011137110826
845150LV00008B/2383

* 9 7 8 1 4 1 8 1 9 4 3 9 0 *